SHATTERED HEART

S.ELAINE.PAUL

Made with ♥ on the Notion Press Platform
www.notionpress.com

Contents

1. CONTENTS

Chapter2

3. UNSPOKEN WORDS

You never touched me

Nor I did

But I felt a serenity

When you touched my soul without using your hands

It will dwell with me last a lifetime

Maybe we were destined to meet

But not to be one

Thus,I set you free

Don't come to me anymore

If my memories wake you up in the mid-night,

Then ceased them

Don't say me to stay anymore

Because sometimes endings are beautiful

Just like autumn leaves

Burn all the pages of Reminiscene

And don't look at back those

Never summon up that memories

Maybe I was the only one

Who always cared

You didn't even do

And I am writing this now

Thinking about you

And maybe you thinking about
Someone else .

Chapter4

Enter Caption

5. IS THAT FUCKIN' LOVE

I forgave you even when I saw you with someone else

Just because seeing you happy

Also makes me happy

I forgave you even after seeing your lip brushes another

Just because seeing you happy

Makes me happy

After seeing your skin touch another

I forget that & still love you fulliest

Just because seeing you happy

makes me happy

You showed me empathy

By told me 'Just be friends'

But believe me dear no need to did this

Because maybe I didn't want that

I may not be your first

But want to be your last, everything

But maybe you aren't in my destiny

Or god doesn't want to keep you in my life

Then why does god send some people into our lives

who won't last forever

Maybe forever was a word meant

for memories,not people.

I ain't marking any on alligation on you
That why you love someone else not me
I just want to ask you that 'why do you came to me and start
that convo'?
Why that fuckin' eye contact happened?
Why?Why?
Or why we met ?
My soul died many days ago
The day we separated from each other
I made that separation by having that thought
that yourn't soluberious for me
Now the outer part of my body just live
Now nothing excites me nor makes me sad
Just an empty soul
Maybe you were the one of the reason of my smile
And to you someone else is the reason behind your smile
Now I'm just waiting for the day when I can leave you from
my mentality too..
I know i am so fool that's why i am writing this
for that person
Who will never know
I never want something from you
All I want is to die in our arm
So come and give me poison
Because I don't want to live anymore
It will becoming very hard for me to pass days
with these wounds.

Goodbye.

Chapter6

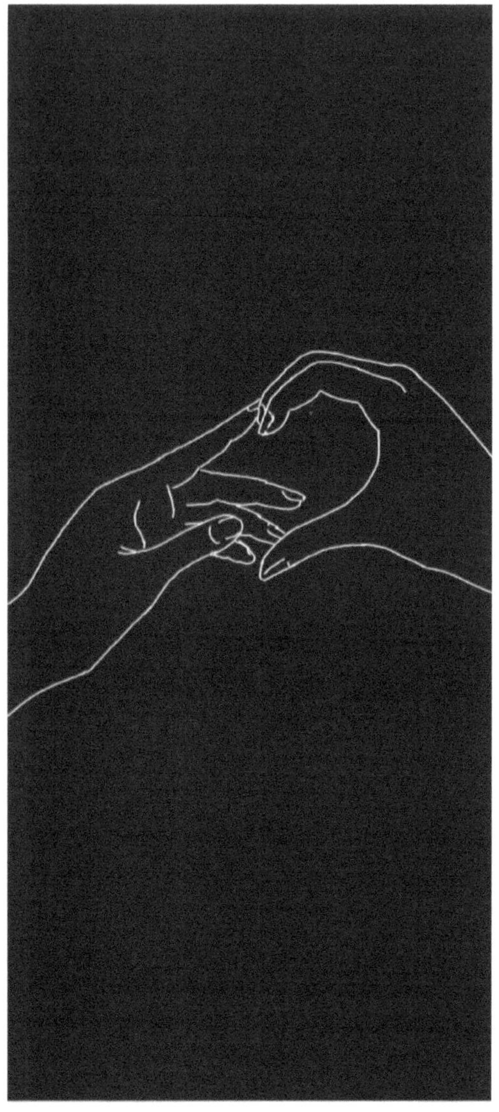

Enter Caption

S.ELAINE.PAUL

7. BLEEDING LOVE

I feel my mind is slowly fadin'

Run over the past thought

when you was trying your girl hiding'

Now I'm replaced by you

Not answering my texts

Is that another cue?

You are a bad liar

When you told me

I'm irreplaceable

FUCK!

I don't need your love ,maligner

Ooh, and now i know

What love is

and I know it ain't for you sure

You'd rather something toxic

So,I poison myself again,again

Till I feel nothing

In my soul

I'm on the edge of something breaking

Yes,I was never there (src:The Weeknd's song)

You made a really deep cut

Poison is spreading in vain

You become the reason why I hate men

Blood is dripping from my hands onto the rose .

Chapter8

Enter Caption

9. ON A RAINY DAY

A room full of darkness

Only a candle lights the room

The wind is blowing cold outside

Sipping into coffee

With this view, I started writing

About my blurry ,wild memory

The weather reminds

About our time

Where you used to stay by my side

This room has a lot of memories of us

Do you remember those days ?

When we were staying

Under the same blanket

Those guilty nights

Blurry minds

That touched me that night

A glass of wine & everything

I wish these would happen

But these all happen in my imagination.

Chapter10

Enter Caption

11. I LOVE YOU?

How can tears drop from the eyes?

How can I cry?

How can you break a heart twice ?

So you might be happy now

After seeing me in pain

I lost you but found me , so it's my gain

I LOVE YOU

LOVE = Longer obsession with a void enemy

Was it my fault that I loved you ?

So in return , do I deserve this ?

That much hatred

How do you sleep peacefully?

Don't you feel guilty ?

How could you be selfish?

Or were you like that ?

But I didn't recognise

Love is not for you

You deserve to be alone

As everyone left ,

To me , it's always been you

But you never cared

Why?

Don't you want love ?

Didn't I treat you special?

Didn't we stay together

What was the imperfection in my love?

Say ..

Why have you done this to me ?

Just because you wanted a physical relationship

Or

Chapter12

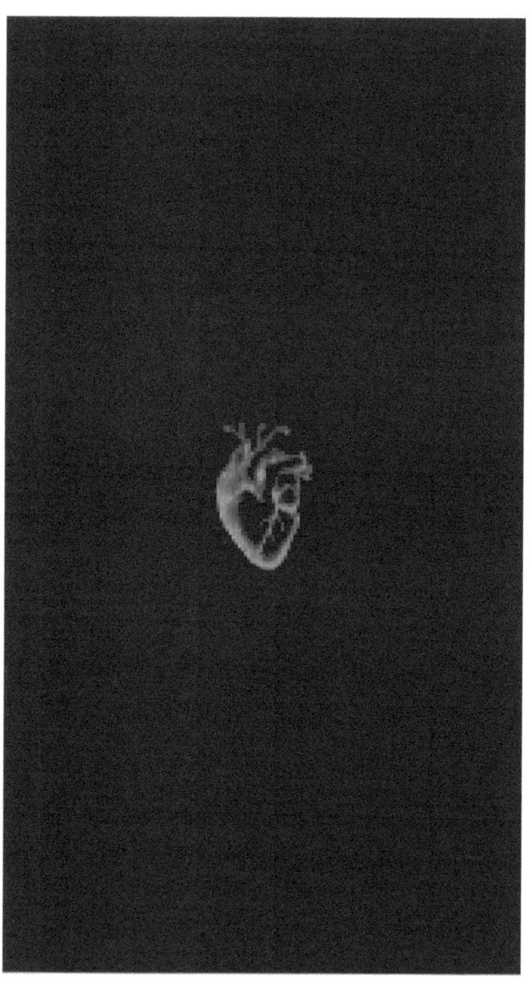

Enter Caption

13. ABOUT THE AUTHOR

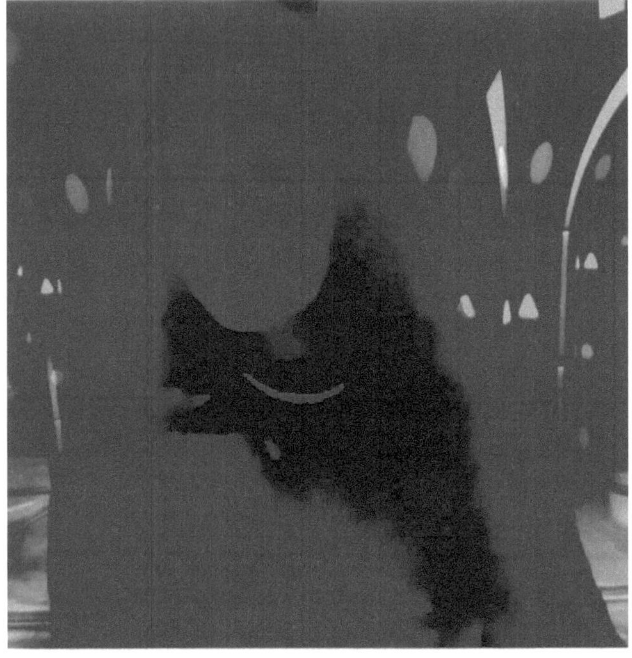

Writer, essayist,enthusiastic and poet **S.Elaine,Paul** was born and grew up in kolkata. She is passionate about writing .Accoustomed to being around primarily adults,she was always mature for her age .From vchildhood she has been reading so many writer's book .

Chapter14

Enter Caption

Chapter15

THANK YOU